WILDLIFE WORLDS

ASIA

TIM HARRIS

CRABTREE
PUBLISHING COMPANY
WWW.CRABTREEBOOKS.COM

CRABTREE
PUBLISHING COMPANY
WWW.CRABTREEBOOKS.COM

Published in Canada
Crabtree Publishing
616 Welland Avenue
St. Catharines, ON
L2M 5V6

Published in the United States
Crabtree Publishing
PMB 59051
350 Fifth Ave, 59th Floor
New York, NY 10118

Published in 2020 by Crabtree Publishing Company

First published in Great Britain in 2019 by The Watts Publishing Group
Copyright © The Watts Publishing Group 2019

Printed in the U.S.A./122019/CG20191101

With thanks to the Nature Picture Library

Author: Tim Harris

Editorial director: Kathy Middleton

Editors: Amy Pimperton, Robin Johnson

Series Designer: Nic Davies smartdesignstudio.co.uk

Photo researchers: Rachelle Morris (Nature Picture Library),
  Laura Sutherland (Nature Picture Library), Diana Morris

Proofreader: Wendy Scavuzzo

Production coordinator and prepress: Tammy McGarr

Print coordinator: Katherine Berti

Photo credits:
Dreamstime:Agami Photo Agency 3b,7b; Carl99 back cover tcl,16-17c; Nico Smit 21b.
Nature PL: Aflo 2b, 13b, 26-27c; Franco Banfi 8, 19cr; Gertrud & Helmut Denzau 23tr; Hanne & Jens Eriksen 29tr, 29c; David Fleethan 9b; Nick Garbutt front cover b; Edwin Giesbers front cover t; Sergey Gorshkov 6c,7t; Graeme Guy/BIA 25tr; Alex Hyde 10-11b; Olga Kamenskaya 18bl, 19br; Tim Laman 21tr; Valeriy Maleev 15c,15b; Gavin Maxwell 27tl; Konstantin Mikhailov 15tl; Constantinos Petrinos 9tl; David Pike 12c; Michael Pitts 16b; Fiona Rogers 11tr; Andy Rouse 24c, 24bl; Roland Seitre 17tr; Markus Varesvuo 13tl; Theo Webb 25b; Staffan Widstrand 27tr.
Shutterstock: Zakirov Aleksey 3t, 18-19c; brnitat 23; brsbw18 17; Butterfly Hunter 6t;Dmussman 1,13tr, 32b; David Evison 11br; ExOrzist back cover tr; frantisekhojdysz backcover tc, 2t,9tr; Andrei Gilbert 19bc; Yann Hunbert 6b; Daniel Karflik 3bg, 4-5bg,14, 31bg; Louie Lea 28c; Wang LiQuang 19tr; Phil MacDPhoto 27bl,32t; Matulee 5; Mazur Travel: 4c,11tc,30b; Meoita 29br; Mirinae front cover c; Tom B Payne 29bl;Dmitry Pichugin 15tr; Meet Podar 21tl; Ondrej Prosicky 4b; Ais Qocak 23tc;Matyas Rehak 20, 31c; Andreas Rose 27br; Salparadis back cover tl, 11tl;Signature Message 3c, 17bl; Vladimir Wrangel 21c, 23cr, 30t; Andrea Zangrilli 22-23c;Milan Zygmunt 25tl.
CC Wikimedia Commons/Peeliden 12.

Library and Archives Canada Cataloguing in Publication

Title: Asia / Tim Harris.
Names: Harris, Tim (Ornithologist), author.
Description: Series statement: Wildlife worlds |
  Previously published: London: Franklin Watts, 2019. | Includes index.
Identifiers: Canadiana (print) 20190200596 |
  Canadiana (ebook) 2019020060X |
  ISBN 9780778776789 (hardcover) |
  ISBN 9780778776840 (softcover) |
  ISBN 9781427125323 (HTML)
Subjects: LCSH: Animals—Asia—Juvenile literature. |
  LCSH: Habitat (Ecology)—Asia—Juvenile literature. | LCSH: Natural
  history—Asia—Juvenile literature. | LCSH: Asia—Juvenile literature.
Classification: LCC QL300 .H37 2020 | DDC j591.95—dc23

Library of Congress Cataloging-in-Publication Data

Names: Harris, Tim (Ornithologist), author.
Title: Asia / Tim Harris.
Description: New York : Crabtree Publishing Company, 2020. |
  Series: Wildlife worlds | Includes index.
Identifiers: LCCN 2019043605 (print) | LCCN 2019043606 (ebook) |
  ISBN 9780778776789 (hardcover) |
  ISBN 9780778776840 (paperback) |
  ISBN 9781427125323 (ebook)
Subjects: LCSH: Animals--Asia--Juvenile literature. | Plants--Asia--Juvenile
  literature.
Classification: LCC QL300 .H37 2020 (print) | LCC QL300 (ebook) |
  DDC 591.95--dc23
LC record available at https://lccn.loc.gov/2019043605
LC ebook record available at https://lccn.loc.gov/2019043606

Contents

Asian Continent

Asia is the largest continent on Earth. It stretches from the Arctic Ocean in the north to the Indian Ocean in the south, and from the Ural Mountains in the west to the Pacific Ocean in the east. Asia has a greater variety of landscapes than any other continent. There is frozen **tundra** in Siberia, a vast **desert** on the Arabian **Peninsula**, and **tropical rain forest** in Malaysia, Indonesia, and Thailand.

Asia also has mangrove forests, wetlands, huge cave systems, **coral reefs**, and vast areas of grassland called steppes. With such a wide range of environments, it is no surprise that the plant and animal life on the continent is also varied. Many animals, including tigers, South Asian river dolphins, giant pandas, and Asian elephants live in the wild only in Asia.

The **corpse** lily is found on the islands of Sumatra and Borneo.

BENGAL TIGER

Asia's longest rivers, the Yangtze and the Yellow, are found in China.

At 29,029 feet (8,848 m), Mount Everest in the Himalayas is the highest mountain in the world.

Giant pandas live in forests in the mountains of China. They spend most of their time eating woody grasses called bamboo.

The Dead Sea Depression is 1,355 feet (413 m) below sea level.

Arctic Circle

Russia

Russia

Ural Mountains

Kamchatka Peninsula

Lake Baikal

Sea of Okhotsk

Caucasus Mountains

Khongoryn Els

Caspian Sea

Gobi Desert

Yellow River

Japan

China

Himalayas

Ranthambore

Mount Fuji

Arabian Desert

India

Yangtze River

South China Karst

Arabian Peninsula

Al-Hajar Mountains

Sundarbans Mangroves

Pacific Ocean

Arabian Sea

Bay of Bengal

Philippines

Ganges River

Thailand

Tubbataha Reef

Malaysia

Equator

Sumatra

Indonesia

Indian Ocean

Borneo Rain Forest

Kamchatka Peninsula

The Kamchatka Peninsula is a land of snow-capped volcanoes that sits between the mighty Pacific Ocean and the Sea of Okhotsk in the far east of Russia.

Wildlife is **abundant** on the peninsula. Brown bears roam the tundra, woodlands, and meadows. Lynx, foxes, wolves, and sables hunt hares, mouselike lemmings, and squirrels called marmots. Thousands of seabirds nest on coastal cliffs and feed on fish from the ocean, where whales, dolphins, and seals live.

Kamchatka is known as the "land of fire and ice." It is the most volcanic part of Asia and 29 of its 160 volcanoes, including the Tolbachik volcanoes (above), are active. The region is bitterly cold for much of the year and is covered with snow and ice.

The rare spoon-billed sandpiper sweeps its unique beak from side to side through the water as it feeds.

Sables are related to weasels and otters. They spend most of their time in the branches of trees.

Humpback whales dive up to 656 feet (200 m) underwater in search of **krill** and small fish to eat.

In winter, Steller's sea eagles hunt for fish from the sea ice that floats on the water around the peninsula.

Tubbataha Reef

The Tubbataha Reef system lies to the west of the islands of the Philippines. It was discovered in the 1970s and is now known as one of the most remarkable reefs in the world.

SEA FAN

The Tubbataha Reef is a rainbow of color. More than 350 different kinds of hard and soft coral (including sea fans) and almost 500 types of fish (including the **endangered** Napoleon wrasse) are found there. Sharks and sea turtles visit the reef in search of meals. There are two coral **atolls** where the reef rises above the water's surface. There, seabirds nest on beaches of white sand.

NAPOLEON WRASSE

The body of the greater blue-ringed octopus is no bigger than a golf ball, but this animal has a deadly **venomous** bite. When threatened, the rings on its skin flash bright blue as a warning to **predators**.

Hammerhead sharks are some of the many creatures that visit the reef. Their wide-set eyes allow these sharks to see all around their bodies.

Borneo Rain Forest

One of the world's oldest rain forests covers much of Borneo, Asia's biggest island. Although many trees have been cut down for their valuable wood, large parts of the rain forest are still unexplored.

More than 3,000 different kinds of trees make up the Borneo rain forest, some growing 164 feet (50 m) tall. They provide homes for an amazing variety of animals, many of which live nowhere else on Earth. There are apes, monkeys, rhinos, elephants, clouded leopards, and bats in the forest. Hundreds of bird and amphibian species live there, as well as thousands of different kinds of insects.

The forest is very **dense**. Fallen trees and thick, tangled vines make it hard for people to walk through. Colorful butterflies flutter through clearings in the forest, hornbills fly from tree to tree in search of fruit. At dusk, bats called flying foxes flap above the **canopy**, where orangutans feed on leaves.

Huntsman spiders rest on trees while they wait to **ambush** their insect **prey**.

The corpse lily is named for its disgusting smell. The smell attracts flies that help **pollinate** the flowers. Its flower is the largest of any plant, growing up to 3 feet (1 m) across.

Orangutans are the most **solitary** of the great apes. These highly intelligent animals build nests made of branches and leaves for sleeping high in the trees.

The rhinoceros hornbill has a hollow horn-like part called a casque on its beak that helps make the bird's calls louder.

11

Mount Fuji

At 12,388 feet (3,776 m), Mount Fuji is the highest peak in Japan. This **dormant** volcano is a very important part of Japanese culture and tradition, and is considered to be one of the country's **sacred** mountains.

Fuji's higher slopes are **barren** and often blanketed with snow, but the lower slopes are covered in **broad-leaved** and **coniferous** forest. Black bears, foxes, and goat antelope called Japanese serows live in the forest. In spring, it echoes with birds singing.

The Japanese emperor butterfly is the national butterfly of Japan.

Spotted nutcrackers live in conifers, where there are plenty of pine nuts for them to eat.

Japanese macaques are intelligent, bold, and often unafraid of people. In winter, they warm themselves in hot volcanic pools.

Cherry blossoms bloom on the lower slopes of Mount Fuji in spring. The cherry blossoms are spectacular and a favorite food of Japanese macaques.

13

Gobi Desert

Northern China and southern Mongolia share the Gobi Desert, the largest desert in Asia. It is very dry there because the high Tibetan **Plateau** to the south prevents rain from reaching the area. On a summer day it may be hot, but at night the temperature often plunges well below freezing.

KHONGORYN ELS

Much of the Gobi is bare rock, with cliffs and steep-sided canyons. Other areas are grassy or covered with saxaul shrubs. Although there is no water in the desert, and it can be baking hot or bitterly cold, many animals can survive in these harsh conditions. Camels, gazelles, and even snow leopards live there.

There are some massive sand **dunes** in the Gobi Desert, such as the Khongoryn Els, which are 112 miles (180 km) long and 984 feet (300 m) high. They are known as Duut Mankhan or Singing Dunes, for the sound the sand makes as the wind blows it.

14

Wild onions are a food source for many animals in the desert.

A Bactrian camel is known for its distinctive two humps. This type of camel is very rare in the wild because most have been raised by people to do work.

Long-eared jerboas hop fast on their long hind legs. They have excellent hearing and their big ears help them lose heat on hot days.

During the day, long-eared hedgehogs rest in holes they dig or take over from other animals. They come out at night to feed on insects and lizards.

South China Karst

When rain and rivers **dissolve limestone**, it creates an amazing landscape called karst. The city of Guilin in southern China is famous for its karst formations.

Water has shaped limestone that is more than 300 million years old into **pinnacles**, rock bridges, cliffs, and canyons. Huge caves have been formed by underground rivers. Many different kinds of animals that live in these caves are nowhere else on Earth. They include fish, bats, and cave crickets. Above ground, a variety of animals make their homes in the forests.

16

Chinese pangolins are covered by rows of overlapping scales that help protect these unusual animals from predators.

Rock towers and cones rise 984 feet (300 m) above the plain like giant teeth. Incredibly, trees grow on the nearly **vertical** cliff faces.

Great roundleaf bats live alone or in small groups in caves. They use **echolocation** to hunt insects at night.

Although Asian golden cats climb well, they spend most of their time on the ground.

Male long-tailed silver pheasants have striking feathers.

Lake Baikal

There is more water in Russia's Lake Baikal than in all of North America's Great Lakes combined. Not only is it the largest freshwater lake by volume on Earth, it also the deepest, plunging to 5,387 feet (1,642 m). Its surface waters freeze each winter.

The clear waters of this ancient lake are home to many fish, including golomyankas, which thrive even at the greatest depths. There are also seals, waterbirds, **crustaceans**, freshwater snails, and even sponges. Surrounding the lake is coniferous forest, where brown bears, wolves, elk, wild boars, and chipmunks live.

BAIKAL SPONGE

Lake Baikal first formed more than 25 million years ago in a deep rift valley, where Earth's **crust** was pulling apart. The lake increases in width by about 1 inch (2 cm) every year.

18

Each year, Siberian rubythroats return to the area around the lake to breed. They leave for their winter habitats in Southeast Asia in September.

Many of the crustaceans found there, such as this amphipod, are **native** to Lake Baikal.

Baikal black grayling swim in shallow water close to the lakeshore.

Baikal seals **bask** on the shores of the lake when they are not fishing in its waters.

Sundarbans Mangroves

The Sundarbans is the world's largest mangrove forest. It stretches across the vast **delta** of the Ganges and Brahmaputra rivers, on the border between Bangladesh and India.

The mixing of the Bay of Bengal's salt water with the fresh river water has created a place of incredible diversity. Crocodiles, turtles, and fish swim in the creeks, and birds called kingfishers perch overhead, looking for unsuspecting fish. Mongooses, fishing cats, and chital deer feed in the dense mangroves where the Bengal tiger, an **apex predator**, hunts its prey.

Unlike most trees, mangroves can grow in the salty seawater that floods the delta's creeks and channels at every high **tide**.

Thousands of people are bitten by the venomous common krait every year. These snakes are often found close to water.

When the tide is low, fiddler crabs scurry across the muddy banks of creeks.

Fishing cats sometimes dive into water to catch fish. They can swim long distances and can even swim underwater.

Chital deer rest in the shade during the hottest part of the day. They come out to feed in the early morning and evening when it is cooler.

Ganges River

The mighty Ganges River carries **snowmelt** from its **glaciers** in the Himalaya Mountains, **monsoon** rain from the Indian plains, and water from countless large and small rivers and streams that flow into it. Only the Amazon and Congo rivers carry more water to the ocean.

After a journey of more than 1,550 miles (2,500 km), the Ganges River passes through the world's largest delta to the Bay of Bengal. Deer, wild boars, and jackals come to its banks to drink, where they are watched by crocodiles on the lookout for a meal. Otters, turtles, and snakes swim in its waters, while herons wade carefully through shallow water, ready to dart forward and grab a passing fish. Birds called kites constantly soar overhead.

Hindus consider the Ganges River to be sacred. It supports millions of people and an amazing variety of wildlife, including endangered reptiles called gharials.

Brahminy kites feed on dead fish and crabs that litter the sides of the river.

Only a few hundred gharials remain in the Ganges. These long-snouted crocodiles eat fish.

Spotted pond turtles swim in search of snails and insect larvae to eat.

After a fishing trip, an Oriental darter spreads its wings to dry them.

Ranthambore

Once a place where the wealthy princes of Jaipur hunted tigers, India's Ranthambore is now a national park where these big cats are protected.

With a mixture of broad-leaved forests, grasslands, wetlands, and many lakes, the park is an exceptional place for wildlife. Tigers are the main attraction, but there are also leopards, hyenas, macaques, crocodiles, snakes, and more than 300 kinds of birds, including thousands of waterbirds.

BENGAL TIGER

Tigers hunt in the forest surrounding the ruins of Ranthambore fort. It is considered a dry forest because it receives rain only during the monsoon.

Mugger crocodiles eat any animals, dead or alive, they can get their jaws around.

White-throated kingfishers dive into water for fish. Both males and females have spectacular feathers. Their unique call sounds a little like laughter.

An Indian peacock with its tail spread is an amazing sight.

Himalayas

The Himalayas are the highest mountain range in the world, with more than 50 peaks topping 23,600 feet (7,200 m). They run 1,400 miles (2,300 km) from Bhutan in the east to northern Pakistan in the west.

MOUNT EVEREST

High in the mountains, hundreds of glaciers carry ice down deep, steep-sided valleys below barren peaks. Fast-flowing rivers tumble over rocks, with pools providing homes for fish and waterbirds. At lower **altitudes**, meadow grasses and wildflowers grow on the mountain slopes in spring and summer. Lower still, the grassland is replaced by forest, where bears, deer, and many other animals live.

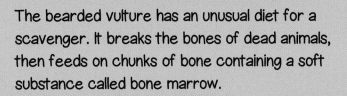

The Himalayan jumping spider lives at altitudes up to 22,000 feet (6,700 m). It is one of the highest-dwelling animals on Earth.

The bearded vulture has an unusual diet for a scavenger. It breaks the bones of dead animals, then feeds on chunks of bone containing a soft substance called bone marrow.

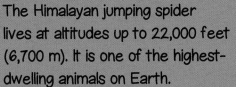

In spring, Himalayan blue poppies flower in high meadows.

Snow leopards are solitary animals that live on high rocky mountain slopes. The markings on their fur help these wild cats blend into the landscape.

Al-Hajar Mountains

Hot, almost lifeless desert covers most of the Arabian Peninsula. Some rain falls in the Al-Hajar Mountains of Oman, however, allowing plants and animals to thrive in this part of the peninsula.

Jebel Shams is the highest peak in the Al-Hajar Mountains, rising to just over 9,840 feet (3,000 m). It overlooks a deep canyon and provides spectacular views of an imposing mountain called Jebel Misht (below).

Just enough rain falls between December and March to support the growth of trees in these rugged mountains. Although the mountains are surrounded by barren desert with low shrubs, higher up the slopes there are olive and fig trees, then juniper woodland. There, it is cooler and is home to more animals, including wild goats, gazelles, and a few Arabian leopards, as well as many reptiles and birds.

Like all reptiles, blue-tailed Oman lizards bask in the sun to warm up their bodies.

Breeding male shining sunbirds have feathers that shine in bright sunlight.

The Arabian tahr is a sure-footed wild goat that lives in the mountains.

Honey badgers often kill and eat venomous snakes.

Glossary

abundant Plentiful

altitude The height of an object above sea level

ambush To attack by surprise

apex predator A predator at the top of the food chain

atoll A coral island made up of a reef surrounding a lagoon

barren Having few or no plants

bask To lie in the sunshine

broad-leaved Having wide, flat leaves instead of needles

canopy The highest tree branches in a forest

coniferous Describing evergreen trees that produce cones and have needle-like leaves

coral reef A hard structure in the sea that is made from the remains of dead coral

corpse A dead body

crust Earth's outer layer

crustacean An animal with an external skeleton but no backbone, such as a crab

delta The area where a river drops mud and sand as it enters a lake or ocean

dense Thick with plants growing close together

desert A place that receives little or no rainfall and has few or no plants

dissolve To make part of a liquid

dormant Not active for now

dune A hill of sand piled up by the wind

echolocation Finding out the position of something by measuring the time it takes for an echo to return

endangered At risk of dying out forever

glacier A large body of ice moving slowly down a valley

krill Shrimp-like marine animals

limestone Rock formed from dead sea animals, coral, and shells

monsoon Heavy seasonal rains in South Asia

native Living or growing naturally in an area

peninsula A piece of land that is almost totally surrounded by water, but is not quite an island

pinnacle A high, pointed piece of rock

plateau High, level ground

pollinate To carry pollen from one flower to another, allowing seeds to be made

predators Animals that hunt and eat other animals

prey Animals that are eaten by other animals

rain forest A dense forest that receives a high amount of rainfall

sacred Connected to a god or religion

snowmelt Water that comes from melted snow

solitary Living alone

tide The changing water level in oceans

tropical Relating to the tropics, the areas above and below the equator

tundra A flat, treeless region of the Arctic where the ground is frozen for most of the year

venomous Producing chemicals that can injure or kill prey

vertical Straight up

Further Information

Books

Auld, Mary. *Pathways Through Asia*. Crabtree Publishing, 2019.

Rockett, Paul. *Mapping Asia*. Crabtree Publishing, 2017.

Son, John. *Asia*. Children's Press, 2019.

Wang, Andrea. *Learning about Asia*. Lerner Publishing, 2016.

Websites

www.dkfindout.com/us/earth/continents/asia/
Lots of interesting and fun facts about Asia.

www.ducksters.com/geography/asia.php
This website has profiles of every country in Asia.

http://gowild.wwf.org.uk/asia
Discover more about Asia with these WWF fact files, stories, games and activities.

www.nationalgeographic.com/animals/index/
Type in the names of animals and get lots of fascinating facts about mammals, reptiles, amphibians, fish, and birds.

Index